College and University Track, Cross-Country and Indoor Attendance and Scorekeeping Information Log

David Thompson

authorHOUSE®

AuthorHouse™
1663 Liberty Drive
Bloomington, IN 47403
www.authorhouse.com
Phone: 1 (800) 839-8640

Published by AuthorHouse 08/09/2018

ISBN: 978-1-5462-5372-3 (sc)
ISBN: 978-1-5462-5371-6 (e)

Library of Congress Control Number: 2018909119

Print information available on the last page.

This book is printed on acid-free paper.

Illustrations by Michael Gillespie

Introduction

Here is how you use this book. It is intended to help coaches and athletes to take attendance and keep scores and maintain statistics for the season and other uses.

I think keeping all the information and scores in one book for the season would be really cool for statistics. This book also provides a Track and Field Code of Ethics, how to score Track and Field Dual Meets, and how to score a Cross-country Meet.

It also includes Outdoor Track Meet Order of Events scoring sheets, Field Event scoring sheet for both indoor and outdoor, Cross-country scoring sheets, Indoor Track Meet Order of Events scoring sheets, Athletes' Prayers, Diet and Nutrition guidelines, and a history of outdoor track. This book is designed for track and field athletes at both men's and women's colleges.

This scorekeeping information log for Track and Field can help you to establish a better program in every way. I think every college and university track, Cross-country and indoor track coach in the United States and Canada should get a copy of this book, because it will help coaches be more structured and coordinated. Thank you for using this book.

Contents

Track and Cross-Country Code of Ethics for Students

Introduction

I know that as a student, I will be required to do whatever I can, whenever I can to take this course and its training seriously. I am committed to outperforming my best.

I will attend all practices. If I cannot be at practice, I will have informed my coach as soon as possible.

I acknowledge hereby, that as a student and athlete of this prestigious institution, I have significant responsibilities. I am among the most visible students on campus; therefore, it is my responsibility to be exemplary. I am expected to behave as an exemplary member of any intercollegiate team and in perfect cohesion with the policy and conduct of this institution. Because athletes are made to uphold the standards of conduct, I will represent this prestigious institution in a manner that would do society and the institution proud. I promise to conduct myself with honesty, integrity and respect for all others at all times.

Code of Conduct

By signing below, I agree to conduct myself the best that I can in a way that would not breach any rules and requirements of the NCAA, the athletic conference in which the team participates, as well as the requirements of my institution. I also agree to the following:

University Community: I shall be an exemplary member of the University community. I shall represent my team inside and outside the classroom while displaying the utmost respect for all members of the University, and conduct myself as my society deems well. I will lead by example. I will remember that both my own and my team's reputations are at stake when I am participating in intercollegiate competition, attending classes, and socializing with friends and others both inside and outside of the University community.

1. **Academic Standing**: I will be fully responsible for my academic progress and achievement. I will make every effort to maintain a respectable and decent standing among my fellow students at the University. I will attend all classes the course has to offer, unless excused for team travel and competition, or if asked or in the case of a serious problem. I know I will be allowed to seek additional academic help to cope with the academic pressures and maintain my academic standing.

2. **Travel as a University Ambassador**: When traveling for competitions or training as a representative of both the institution and my team, I will behave responsibly and portray a positive image of the institution at all times.

3. **Cyberspace**: I will not be associated with authoring, forwarding, or posting vulgar or offensive notes, texts, photographs, or other content that can possibly reflect negatively on me, my team, or the institution. Whenever possible, I will discourage others from posting texts or photographs that could be deemed unflattering or damaging to my reputation, or that of others, or to the reputations of the team or the institution. I acknowledge that I am required to comply with the Rules and Guidelines for Student-Athlete Use of Social Media.

4. **Alcohol and Drug Use:** I will not partake in the consumption of alcoholic beverages on team trips or athletic events, as they are prohibited as per athletic usage. I will comply with the policies described in the institution's Statement on Illegal Drugs and Alcohol.

5. **Violence**: I will not partake and will not tolerate any act of violence, including assaults on persons or property, hate crimes, stalking, sexual violence or any other conduct that is considered prohibited or unadvisable by law or Institutional policy. I acknowledge that the Department of Athletics may, in its discretion, immediately suspend me from my team and prohibit me from practice and competition until further notice in case I'm accused or found guilty of violence or sexual misconduct.

6. **Nonconsensual Sexual Contact**: I will not partake in any nonconsensual sexual contact. I acknowledge that all forms of harassment and nonconsensual sexual contact are prohibited, both by law and this institution's rules, described in more detail in the Sexual Harassment Policy that should be present in every student handbook.

7. **Hazing:** I will not willingly participate in hazing of any sort. I acknowledge that such acts are may result in severance of connection with membership on an institution athletic team and participation in an informal or formal team activity, and are strictly prohibited.

8. **Remaining Informed of Expectations and Policies:** I am considered and will be responsible for my own behavior, for reading, understanding, and abiding by the policies applicable to me, as referred to in the current year's Student-Athlete Handbook.

9. **General Conduct**: I will refrain from any act, whether physical, mental, emotional or psychological, that subjects another person, voluntarily or involuntarily, to anything that may abuse, mistreat, degrade, humiliate, harass, or intimidate another person. Such acts may include, but are not limited to: forcing, requiring, or pressuring others to consume alcohol or any other substance; forcing, requiring, or pressuring others to involuntarily perform physical activities or to tattoo, pierce or shave any part of the body; forcing, requiring, or pressuring others to take part in an illegal or indecent activity; disturbing others during normal sleeping hours; or physically abusing others in any way.

If I have breaches to the Code of Conduct, any of the articles mentioned above as per the institution's agreement, I will be asked to leave the spot reserved for me on my team.

I hereby agree to all the articles of the above document, which can be altered as per institutional policy or by the amendments made to it by the relevant authorities.

_____ Athlete's signature
_____ Date

Track and Field Season

Track and Field Attendance Calendar

Month: _____   Coach: _____

Date: _____   Season: _____

Student Name	M	Tu	W	Th	F	Sa	Su	M	Tu	W	Th	F	Sa	Su	M	Tu	W	Th	F	Sa	Su	M	Tu	W	Th	F	Sa	Su	T	U	E	P

Enter: T=Tardy, U=Unexcused, E=Excused , P=Present   Totals

David Thompson

Track and Field Attendance Calendar

Month: _____   Coach: _____

Date: _____   Season: _____

Student Name	M	Tu	W	Th	F	Sa	Su	M	Tu	W	Th	F	Sa	Su	M	Tu	W	Th	F	Sa	Su	M	Tu	W	Th	F	Sa	Su	T	U	E	P

Enter: T=Tardy, U=Unexcused, E=Excused, P=Present — Totals

6

Track and Field Attendance Calendar

Month: _____   Coach: _____

Date: _____   Season: _____

Student Name	M	Tu	W	Th	F	Sa	Su	M	Tu	W	Th	F	Sa	Su	M	Tu	W	Th	F	Sa	Su	M	Tu	W	Th	F	Sa	Su	T	U	E	P

Enter: T=Tardy, U=Unexcused, E=Excused, P=Present — Totals

David Thompson

Track and Field Attendance Calendar

Month: _____   Coach: _____

Date: _____   Season: _____

Student Name	M	Tu	W	Th	F	Sa	Su	M	Tu	W	Th	F	Sa	Su	M	Tu	W	Th	F	Sa	Su	M	Tu	W	Th	F	Sa	Su	T	U	E	P

Enter: T=Tardy, U=Unexcused, E=Excused, P=Present   Totals

Track and Field Attendance Calendar

Month: _____   Coach: _____

Date: _____   Season: _____

	Enter: T=Tardy, U=Unexcused, E=Excused , P=Present																												Totals			
Student Name	M	Tu	W	Th	F	Sa	Su	M	Tu	W	Th	F	Sa	Su	M	Tu	W	Th	F	Sa	Su	M	Tu	W	Th	F	Sa	Su	T	U	E	P

Track and Field Attendance Calendar

Month: _____   Coach: _____

Date: _____   Season: _____

Student Name	M	Tu	W	Th	F	Sa	Su	M	Tu	W	Th	F	Sa	Su	M	Tu	W	Th	F	Sa	Su	M	Tu	W	Th	F	Sa	Su	T	U	E	P

Enter: T=Tardy, U=Unexcused, E=Excused, P=Present   Totals

Track and Field Scoring—Dual Meets

Scoring in a track dual meet is calculated on a points basis. Generally, the first three places in an event will score points for the team. A first-place finish is awarded 5 points, a second-place finish is awarded 3 points, and a third-place finish is awarded 1 point.

For example, if Anthony Brown of Springfield takes first place in the 400 meters, he earns 5 points for his team. If the competitors from Westfield take second and third place, they would earn 4 points; that is, 3 points for second place plus 1 point for third place.

The exception to this is in the relays. In this case, first place is awarded 5 points, but there are no points awarded for second place. As the meet progresses, the points are tallied as each event is completed, and a running tally is kept until the final score.

A partial example of a track and field score sheet is shown here:

Event	Competitor/College/Time or Mark			Score	
	1st place	2nd place	3rd place	Springfield	Westfield
4 x 100 relay	Springfield 48.22	Westfield 49.88	(no points for 2nd)	5	0
1600 m	Brown OV 4:33.21	Smith W 4:35.77	Tran OV 4:37.29	6/11	3/3
110 H	Garcia OV 15.57	Puchalski OV 16.58	Luu W 18.64	8/19	1/4
400 m	Rivera W 51.32	Singer OV 55.29	Wallis OV 56.27	4/23	5/9
100 m	Fremont OV 11.12	Wasowski OV 11.51	Resendes OV 11.98	9/31	0/9

This will continue for all eight running events, six field events and two relays. Note that every point earned for the team is also a point taken away from the other team, so every point earned is actually a two-point switch.

Taking that further, if a team sweeps an event, such as Springfield did in the 100 meters in the preceding example, the team earns all 9 points awarded for that event. What is just as important is that its competitor, in this case Westfield, will not earn any points. Had Westfield taken those three places, it would have had those 9 points; thus, there would be an 18-point switch in the score.

David Thompson

League Finals and Invitational or Competition Scoring

League Finals are scored through six places, and all six places score points, including relays. The point breakdown for points earned for places is as follows. The score tally is kept just as in dual meets.

1st place = 10 points
2nd place = 8 points
3rd place = 6 points
4th place = 4 points
5th place = 2 points
6th place = 1 point

College and University Outdoor Track Meet - Order of Events

Scoring Results Points

Men/Women _____ / _____

Date: _____

1st place 5pts 2nd place 3pts 3rd place 1pt 5pts 4x400m/4x100m					
Events	**First**	**Second**	**Third**	**Home**	**Visitor**
Hammer					
Javelin					
Shot put					
Pole Vault					
Long Jump					
High Jump					
Triple Jump					
Discus					
10,000 meters					
4x100m Relay					
Steeplechase					
1500m					
100m Hurdle Finals					
110m Hurdle Finals					
400m					
100m Dash Finals					
800m					
400m Hurdles					
200m					
5,000m					
4x400m Relay					
Final score					

David Thompson

College and University Outdoor Track Meet – Order of Events

Scoring Results Points

Men/Women _____ / _____

Date: _____

1ˢᵗ place 5pts 2ⁿᵈ place 3pts 3ʳᵈ place 1pt 5pts 4x400m/4x100m					
Events	**First**	**Second**	**Third**	**Home**	**Visitor**
Hammer					
Javelin					
Shot put					
Pole Vault					
Long Jump					
High Jump					
Triple Jump					
Discus					
10,000 meters					
4x 100m Relay					
Steeplechase					
1500m					
100m Hurdle Finals					
110m Hurdle Finals					
400m					
100m Dash Finals					
800m					
400m Hurdles					
200m					
5,000m					
4x 400m Relay					
Final score					

College and University Outdoor Track Meet - Order of Events

Scoring Results Points

Men/Women _____ / _____

Date: _____

1ˢᵗ place 5pts 2ⁿᵈ place 3pts 3ʳᵈ place 1pt 5pts 4×400m/4×100m					
Events	**First**	**Second**	**Third**	**Home**	**Visitor**
Hammer					
Javelin					
Shot put					
Pole Vault					
Long Jump					
High Jump					
Triple Jump					
Discus					
10,000 meters					
4 x 100m Relay					
Steeplechase					
1500m					
100m Hurdle Finals					
110m Hurdle Finals					
400m					
100m Dash Finals					
800m					
400m Hurdles					
200m					
5,000m					
4 x 400m Relay					
Final score					

College and University Outdoor Track Meet - Order of Events

Scoring Results Points

Men/Women _____ / _____

Date: _____

1st place 5pts 2nd place 3pts 3rd place 1pt 5pts 4x400m/4x100m					
Events	First	Second	Third	Home	Visitor
Hammer					
Javelin					
Shot put					
Pole Vault					
Long Jump					
High Jump					
Triple Jump					
Discus					
10,000 meters					
4x 100m Relay					
Steeplechase					
1500m					
100m Hurdle Finals					
110m Hurdle Finals					
400m					
100m Dash Finals					
800m					
400m Hurdles					
200m					
5,000m					
4x 400m Relay					
Final score					

College and University Outdoor Track Meet – Order of Events

Scoring Results Points

Men/Women _____ / _____

Date: _____

1ˢᵗ place 5pts 2ⁿᵈ place 3pts 3ʳᵈ place 1pt 5pts 4 x 400m/4 x 100m					
Events	**First**	**Second**	**Third**	**Home**	**Visitor**
Hammer					
Javelin					
Shot put					
Pole Vault					
Long Jump					
High Jump					
Triple Jump					
Discus					
10,000 meters					
4 x 100m Relay					
Steeplechase					
1500m					
100m Hurdle Finals					
110m Hurdle Finals					
400m					
100m Dash Finals					
800m					
400m Hurdles					
200m					
5,000m					
4 x 400m Relay					
Final score					

David Thompson

College and University Outdoor Track Meet – Order of Events

Scoring Results Points

Men/Women _____ / _____

Date: _____

1st place 5pts 2nd place 3pts 3rd place 1pt 5pts 4x400m/4x100m					
Events	**First**	**Second**	**Third**	**Home**	**Visitor**
Hammer					
Javelin					
Shot put					
Pole Vault					
Long Jump					
High Jump					
Triple Jump					
Discus					
10,000 meters					
4x 100m Relay					
Steeplechase					
1500m					
100m Hurdle Finals					
110m Hurdle Finals					
400m					
100m Dash Finals					
800m					
400m Hurdles					
200m					
5,000m					
4x 400m Relay					
Final score					

College and University Outdoor Track Meet - Order of Events

Scoring Results Points

Men/Women _____ / _____

Date: _____

1st place 5pts 2nd place 3pts 3rd place 1pt 5pts 4 x 400m/4 x 100m					
Events	**First**	**Second**	**Third**	**Home**	**Visitor**
Hammer					
Javelin					
Shot put					
Pole Vault					
Long Jump					
High Jump					
Triple Jump					
Discus					
10,000 meters					
4 x 100m Relay					
Steeplechase					
1500m					
100m Hurdle Finals					
110m Hurdle Finals					
400m					
100m Dash Finals					
800m					
400m Hurdles					
200m					
5,000m					
4 x 400m Relay					
Final score					

College and University Outdoor Track Meet - Order of Events

Scoring Results Points

Men/Women _____ / _____

Date: _____

1st place 5pts 2nd place 3pts 3rd place 1pt 5pts 4x400m/4x100m					
Events	**First**	**Second**	**Third**	**Home**	**Visitor**
Hammer					
Javelin					
Shot put					
Pole Vault					
Long Jump					
High Jump					
Triple Jump					
Discus					
10,000 meters					
4x 100m Relay					
Steeplechase					
1500m					
100m Hurdle Finals					
110m Hurdle Finals					
400m					
100m Dash Finals					
800m					
400m Hurdles					
200m					
5,000m					
4x 400m Relay					
Final score					

College and University Outdoor Track Meet - Order of Events

Scoring Results Points

Men/Women _____ / _____

Date: _____

1ˢᵗ place 5pts 2ⁿᵈ place 3pts 3ʳᵈ place 1pt 5pts 4 x 400m/4 x 100m					
Events	**First**	**Second**	**Third**	**Home**	**Visitor**
Hammer					
Javelin					
Shot put					
Pole Vault					
Long Jump					
High Jump					
Triple Jump					
Discus					
10,000 meters					
4 x 100m Relay					
Steeplechase					
1500m					
100m Hurdle Finals					
110m Hurdle Finals					
400m					
100m Dash Finals					
800m					
400m Hurdles					
200m					
5,000m					
4 x 400m Relay					
Final score					

College and University Outdoor Track Meet – Order of Events

Scoring Results Points

Men/Women _____ / _____

Date: _____

1st place 5pts 2nd place 3pts 3rd place 1pt 5pts 4x400m/4x100m					
Events	**First**	**Second**	**Third**	**Home**	**Visitor**
Hammer					
Javelin					
Shot put					
Pole Vault					
Long Jump					
High Jump					
Triple Jump					
Discus					
10,000 meters					
4x 100m Relay					
Steeplechase					
1500m					
100m Hurdle Finals					
110m Hurdle Finals					
400m					
100m Dash Finals					
800m					
400m Hurdles					
200m					
5,000m					
4x 400m Relay					
Final score					

College and University Outdoor Track Meet - Order of Events

Scoring Results Points

Men/Women _____ / _____

Date: _____

1st place 5pts 2nd place 3pts 3rd place 1pt 5pts 4x400m/4x100m					
Events	**First**	**Second**	**Third**	**Home**	**Visitor**
Hammer					
Javelin					
Shot put					
Pole Vault					
Long Jump					
High Jump					
Triple Jump					
Discus					
10,000 meters					
4 x 100m Relay					
Steeplechase					
1500m					
100m Hurdle Finals					
110m Hurdle Finals					
400m					
100m Dash Finals					
800m					
400m Hurdles					
200m					
5,000m					
4 x 400m Relay					
Final score					

David Thompson

College and University Outdoor Track Meet - Order of Events

Scoring Results Points

Men/Women _____ / _____

Date: _____

1st place 5pts 2nd place 3pts 3rd place 1pt 5pts 4x400m/4x100m					
Events	First	Second	Third	Home	Visitor
Hammer					
Javelin					
Shot put					
Pole Vault					
Long Jump					
High Jump					
Triple Jump					
Discus					
10,000 meters					
4x 100m Relay					
Steeplechase					
1500m					
100m Hurdle Finals					
110m Hurdle Finals					
400m					
100m Dash Finals					
800m					
400m Hurdles					
200m					
5,000m					
4x 400m Relay					
Final score					

College and University Outdoor Track Meet - Order of Events

Scoring Results Points

Men/Women _____ / _____

Date: _____

1st place 5pts 2nd place 3pts 3rd place 1pt 5pts 4x400m/4x100m					
Events	**First**	**Second**	**Third**	**Home**	**Visitor**
Hammer					
Javelin					
Shot put					
Pole Vault					
Long Jump					
High Jump					
Triple Jump					
Discus					
10,000 meters					
4 x 100m Relay					
Steeplechase					
1500m					
100m Hurdle Finals					
110m Hurdle Finals					
400m					
100m Dash Finals					
800m					
400m Hurdles					
200m					
5,000m					
4 x 400m Relay					
Final score					

College and University Outdoor Track Meet - Order of Events

Scoring Results Points

Men/Women _____ / _____

Date: _____

1st place 5pts 2nd place 3pts 3rd place 1pt 5pts 4x400m/4x100m					
Events	First	Second	Third	Home	Visitor
Hammer					
Javelin					
Shot put					
Pole Vault					
Long Jump					
High Jump					
Triple Jump					
Discus					
10,000 meters					
4x 100m Relay					
Steeplechase					
1500m					
100m Hurdle Finals					
110m Hurdle Finals					
400m					
100m Dash Finals					
800m					
400m Hurdles					
200m					
5,000m					
4x 400m Relay					
Final score					

Athletes Scoring Sheet

Name	Event	Results
1.		
2.		
3.		
4.		
5.		
6.		
7.		
8.		
9.		
10.		
11.		
12.		
13.		
14.		
15.		
16.		
17.		
18.		
19.		
20.		
21.		
22.		
23.		
24.		
25.		
26.		
27.		
28.		
29.		
30.		

Athletes Scoring Sheet

Name	Event	Results
1.		
2.		
3.		
4.		
5.		
6.		
7.		
8.		
9.		
10.		
11.		
12.		
13.		
14.		
15.		
16.		
17.		
18.		
19.		
20.		
21.		
22.		
23.		
24.		
25.		
26.		
27.		
28.		
29.		
30.		

Athletes Scoring Sheet

Name	Event	Results
1.		
2.		
3.		
4.		
5.		
6.		
7.		
8.		
9.		
10.		
11.		
12.		
13.		
14.		
15.		
16.		
17.		
18.		
19.		
20.		
21.		
22.		
23.		
24.		
25.		
26.		
27.		
28.		
29.		
30.		

Athletes Scoring Sheet

Name	Event	Results
1.		
2.		
3.		
4.		
5.		
6.		
7.		
8.		
9.		
10.		
11.		
12.		
13.		
14.		
15.		
16.		
17.		
18.		
19.		
20.		
21.		
22.		
23.		
24.		
25.		
26.		
27.		
28.		
29.		
30.		

Athletes Scoring Sheet

Name	Event	Results
1.		
2.		
3.		
4.		
5.		
6.		
7.		
8.		
9.		
10.		
11.		
12.		
13.		
14.		
15.		
16.		
17.		
18.		
19.		
20.		
21.		
22.		
23.		
24.		
25.		
26.		
27.		
28.		
29.		
30.		

Athletes Scoring Sheet

Name	Event	Results
1.		
2.		
3.		
4.		
5.		
6.		
7.		
8.		
9.		
10.		
11.		
12.		
13.		
14.		
15.		
16.		
17.		
18.		
19.		
20.		
21.		
22.		
23.		
24.		
25.		
26.		
27.		
28.		
29.		
30.		

Athletes Scoring Sheet

Name	Event	Results
1.		
2.		
3.		
4.		
5.		
6.		
7.		
8.		
9.		
10.		
11.		
12.		
13.		
14.		
15.		
16.		
17.		
18.		
19.		
20.		
21.		
22.		
23.		
24.		
25.		
26.		
27.		
28.		
29.		
30.		

Athletes Scoring Sheet

Name	Event	Results
1.		
2.		
3.		
4.		
5.		
6.		
7.		
8.		
9.		
10.		
11.		
12.		
13.		
14.		
15.		
16.		
17.		
18.		
19.		
20.		
21.		
22.		
23.		
24.		
25.		
26.		
27.		
28.		
29.		
30.		

Athletes Scoring Sheet

Name	Event	Results
1.		
2.		
3.		
4.		
5.		
6.		
7.		
8.		
9.		
10.		
11.		
12.		
13.		
14.		
15.		
16.		
17.		
18.		
19.		
20.		
21.		
22.		
23.		
24.		
25.		
26.		
27.		
28.		
29.		
30.		

Athletes Scoring Sheet

Name	Event	Results
1.		
2.		
3.		
4.		
5.		
6.		
7.		
8.		
9.		
10.		
11.		
12.		
13.		
14.		
15.		
16.		
17.		
18.		
19.		
20.		
21.		
22.		
23.		
24.		
25.		
26.		
27.		
28.		
29.		
30.		

Athletes Scoring Sheet

Name	Event	Results
1.		
2.		
3.		
4.		
5.		
6.		
7.		
8.		
9.		
10.		
11.		
12.		
13.		
14.		
15.		
16.		
17.		
18.		
19.		
20.		
21.		
22.		
23.		
24.		
25.		
26.		
27.		
28.		
29.		
30.		

Athletes Scoring Sheet

Name	Event	Results
1.		
2.		
3.		
4.		
5.		
6.		
7.		
8.		
9.		
10.		
11.		
12.		
13.		
14.		
15.		
16.		
17.		
18.		
19.		
20.		
21.		
22.		
23.		
24.		
25.		
26.		
27.		
28.		
29.		
30.		

Field Event Scoring Sheet

Men/Women: _____ Date: _____ .

Long Jump/ Hammer	Triple Jump	Shot Put	Discus	Javelin	High Jump	Pole Vault
Name	School	1st Attempt	2nd Attempt	3rd Attempt	Best	Place
1.						
2.						
3.						
4.						
5.						
6.						
7.						
8.						
9.						
10.						
11.						
12.						
13.						
14.						
15.						
16.						
17.						
18.						
19.						
20.						
21.						
22.						
23.						
24.						
25.						
26.						
27.						
28.						
29.						
30.						

Field Event Scoring Sheet

Men/Women: _____ Date: _____ .

Long Jump/ Hammer	Triple Jump	Shot Put	Discus	Javelin	High Jump	Pole Vault
Name	School	1st Attempt	2nd Attempt	3rd Attempt	Best	Place
1.						
2.						
3.						
4.						
5.						
6.						
7.						
8.						
9.						
10.						
11.						
12.						
13.						
14.						
15.						
16.						
17.						
18.						
19.						
20.						
21.						
22.						
23.						
24.						
25.						
26.						
27.						
28.						
29.						
30.						

Field Event Scoring Sheet

Men/Women: _____ Date: _____ .

Long Jump/ Hammer	Triple Jump	Shot Put	Discus	Javelin	High Jump	Pole Vault
Name	School	1st Attempt	2nd Attempt	3rd Attempt	Best	Place
1.						
2.						
3.						
4.						
5.						
6.						
7.						
8.						
9.						
10.						
11.						
12.						
13.						
14.						
15.						
16.						
17.						
18.						
19.						
20.						
21.						
22.						
23.						
24.						
25.						
26.						
27.						
28.						
29.						
30.						

Field Event Scoring Sheet

Men/Women: _____ Date: _____ .

Long Jump/ Hammer	Triple Jump	Shot Put	Discus	Javelin	High Jump	Pole Vault
Name	**School**	**1ˢᵗ Attempt**	**2ⁿᵈ Attempt**	**3ʳᵈ Attempt**	**Best**	**Place**
1.						
2.						
3.						
4.						
5.						
6.						
7.						
8.						
9.						
10.						
11.						
12.						
13.						
14.						
15.						
16.						
17.						
18.						
19.						
20.						
21.						
22.						
23.						
24.						
25.						
26.						
27.						
28.						
29.						
30.						

Field Event Scoring Sheet

Men/Women: _____ Date: _____ .

Long Jump/ Hammer	Triple Jump	Shot Put	Discus	Javelin	High Jump	Pole Vault
Name	School	1st Attempt	2nd Attempt	3rd Attempt	Best	Place
1.						
2.						
3.						
4.						
5.						
6.						
7.						
8.						
9.						
10.						
11.						
12.						
13.						
14.						
15.						
16.						
17.						
18.						
19.						
20.						
21.						
22.						
23.						
24.						
25.						
26.						
27.						
28.						
29.						
30.						

David Thompson

Field Event Scoring Sheet

Men/Women: _____ Date: _____ .

Long Jump/ Hammer	Triple Jump	Shot Put	Discus	Javelin	High Jump	Pole Vault
Name	School	1ˢᵗ Attempt	2ⁿᵈ Attempt	3ʳᵈ Attempt	Best	Place
1.						
2.						
3.						
4.						
5.						
6.						
7.						
8.						
9.						
10.						
11.						
12.						
13.						
14.						
15.						
16.						
17.						
18.						
19.						
20.						
21.						
22.						
23.						
24.						
25.						
26.						
27.						
28.						
29.						
30.						

Field Event Scoring Sheet

Men/Women: _____ Date: _____ .

Long Jump/ Hammer	Triple Jump	Shot Put	Discus	Javelin	High Jump	Pole Vault
Name	School	1ˢᵗ Attempt	2ⁿᵈ Attempt	3ʳᵈ Attempt	Best	Place
1.						
2.						
3.						
4.						
5.						
6.						
7.						
8.						
9.						
10.						
11.						
12.						
13.						
14.						
15.						
16.						
17.						
18.						
19.						
20.						
21.						
22.						
23.						
24.						
25.						
26.						
27.						
28.						
29.						
30.						

Field Event Scoring Sheet

Men/Women: _____ Date: _____ .

Long Jump/ Hammer	Triple Jump	Shot Put	Discus	Javelin	High Jump	Pole Vault
Name	**School**	**1ˢᵗ Attempt**	**2ⁿᵈ Attempt**	**3ʳᵈ Attempt**	**Best**	**Place**
1.						
2.						
3.						
4.						
5.						
6.						
7.						
8.						
9.						
10.						
11.						
12.						
13.						
14.						
15.						
16.						
17.						
18.						
19.						
20.						
21.						
22.						
23.						
24.						
25.						
26.						
27.						
28.						
29.						
30.						

Field Event Scoring Sheet

Men/Women: _____ Date: _____ .

Long Jump/ Hammer	Triple Jump	Shot Put	Discus	Javelin	High Jump	Pole Vault
Name	School	1st Attempt	2nd Attempt	3rd Attempt	Best	Place
1.						
2.						
3.						
4.						
5.						
6.						
7.						
8.						
9.						
10.						
11.						
12.						
13.						
14.						
15.						
16.						
17.						
18.						
19.						
20.						
21.						
22.						
23.						
24.						
25.						
26.						
27.						
28.						
29.						
30.						

David Thompson

Field Event Scoring Sheet

Men/Women: _____ Date: _____ .

Long Jump/ Hammer	Triple Jump	Shot Put	Discus	Javelin	High Jump	Pole Vault
Name	School	1st Attempt	2nd Attempt	3rd Attempt	Best	Place
1.						
2.						
3.						
4.						
5.						
6.						
7.						
8.						
9.						
10.						
11.						
12.						
13.						
14.						
15.						
16.						
17.						
18.						
19.						
20.						
21.						
22.						
23.						
24.						
25.						
26.						
27.						
28.						
29.						
30.						

Cross-country Season

Cross-country Attendance Calendar
How to Score a Cross-country Meet
College and University Cross-country Score Sheet

Cross Country Attendance Calendar

Month: _____   Coach: _____

Date: _____   Season: _____

Student Name	M	Tu	W	Th	F	Sa	Su	M	Tu	W	Th	F	Sa	Su	M	Tu	W	Th	F	Sa	Su	M	Tu	W	Th	F	Sa	Su	T	U	E	P

Enter: T=Tardy, U=Unexcused, E=Excused, P=Present — Totals

David Thompson

Cross Country Attendance Calendar

Month: _____   Coach: _____

Date: _____   Season: _____

Student Name	Enter: T=Tardy, U=Unexcused, E=Excused , P=Present																												Totals			
	M	Tu	W	Th	F	Sa	Su	M	Tu	W	Th	F	Sa	Su	M	Tu	W	Th	F	Sa	Su	M	Tu	W	Th	F	Sa	Su	T	U	E	P

52

Cross Country Attendance Calendar

Month: _____

Coach: _____

Date: _____

Season: _____

Student Name	Enter: T=Tardy, U=Unexcused, E=Excused , P=Present																												Totals			
	M	Tu	W	Th	F	Sa	Su	M	Tu	W	Th	F	Sa	Su	M	Tu	W	Th	F	Sa	Su	M	Tu	W	Th	F	Sa	Su	T	U	E	P

David Thompson

Cross Country Attendance Calendar

Month: _____   Coach: _____

Date: _____   Season: _____

Student Name	Enter: T=Tardy, U=Unexcused, E=Excused , P=Present																												Totals			
	M	Tu	W	Th	F	Sa	Su	M	Tu	W	Th	F	Sa	Su	M	Tu	W	Th	F	Sa	Su	M	Tu	W	Th	F	Sa	Su	T	U	E	P

Cross Country Attendance Calendar

Month: _____   Coach: _____

Date: _____   Season: _____

Student Name	M	Tu	W	Th	F	Sa	Su	M	Tu	W	Th	F	Sa	Su	M	Tu	W	Th	F	Sa	Su	M	Tu	W	Th	F	Sa	Su	T	U	E	P

Enter: T=Tardy, U=Unexcused, E=Excused, P=Present — Totals

Cross Country Attendance Calendar

Month: _____   Coach: _____

Date: _____   Season: _____

Student Name	M	Tu	W	Th	F	Sa	Su	M	Tu	W	Th	F	Sa	Su	M	Tu	W	Th	F	Sa	Su	M	Tu	W	Th	F	Sa	Su	T	U	E	P

Enter: T=Tardy, U=Unexcused, E=Excused, P=Present — Totals

Cross Country Attendance Calendar

Month: _____   Coach: _____

Date: _____   Season: _____

Student Name	M	Tu	W	Th	F	Sa	Su	M	Tu	W	Th	F	Sa	Su	M	Tu	W	Th	F	Sa	Su	M	Tu	W	Th	F	Sa	Su	T	U	E	P

Enter: T=Tardy, U=Unexcused, E=Excused, P=Present — Totals

David Thompson

Cross Country Attendance Calendar

Month: _____

Date: _____

Coach: _____

Season: _____

Student Name	M	Tu	W	Th	F	Sa	Su	M	Tu	W	Th	F	Sa	Su	M	Tu	W	Th	F	Sa	Su	M	Tu	W	Th	F	Sa	Su	T	U	E	P

Enter: T=Tardy, U=Unexcused, E=Excused, P=Present — Totals

58

How to Score a Cross-country Meet

The first five runners from each team to cross the finish line receive the points that correspond to their place. The first-place runner receives one point, the second-place runner receives two points, and so on. **The team receiving the lowest score wins.**

The sixth and seventh runners on a team, although they don't receive a score, can also be important in that they can "displace" scoring runners from the other team. For example:

	College 1	College 2
	3rd	1st
	4th	2nd
	6th	5th
	7th	11th
	8th	12th
	(9th)	**31**
	(10th)	
Final Score:	**28**	

College 1 wins. As you can see, even though College 1's sixth- and seventh-place runners' scores were not added into the total, they were enough to displace College 2's fourth- and fifth-place runners' scores, to give the win to College 1.

A score of 27 always wins the meet, as does having the first-, second- and third-place winners, with at least five runners finishing. The final instance is called a "sweep."

College and University Cross Country Score Sheet

EVENT _____ **DATE** _____ **Site** _____ **Weather** _____

Condition of Course _____ **Course Distance** _____ **Course Record** _____

Place	Name	Time	Team
1.			
2.			
3.			
4.			
5.			
6.			
7.			
8.			
9.			
10.			
11.			
12.			
13.			
14.			
15.			
16.			
17.			
18.			
19.			
20.			
21.			
22.			
23.			
24.			
25.			
26.			
27.			
28.			
29.			
30.			
31.			
32.			
33.			
34.			
35.			
36.			
37.			
38.			
39.			
40.			

Place	Name	Time	Team
41.			
42.			
43.			
44.			
45.			
46.			
47.			
48.			
49.			
50.			

Team Results

Team		OA Place	Time	Points
1.				
2.				
3.				
4.				
5.				
Total Team Points				
6.				
7.				

Team		OA Place	Time	Points
1.				
2.				
3.				
4.				
5.				
Total Team Points				
6.				
7.				

College and University Cross Country Score Sheet

EVENT _____ DATE _____ Site _____ Weather _____

Condition of Course _____ Course Distance _____ Course Record _____

Place	Name	Time	Team
1.			
2.			
3.			
4.			
5.			
6.			
7.			
8.			
9.			
10.			
11.			
12.			
13.			
14.			
15.			
16.			
17.			
18.			
19.			
20.			
21.			
22.			
23.			
24.			
25.			
26.			
27.			
28.			
29.			
30.			
31.			
32.			
33.			
34.			
35.			
36.			
37.			
38.			
39.			
40.			

Place	Name	Time	Team
41.			
42.			
43.			
44.			
45.			
46.			
47.			
48.			
49.			
50.			

Team Results

Team		OA Place	Time	Points
1.				
2.				
3.				
4.				
5.				
Total Team Points				
6.				
7.				

Team		OA Place	Time	Points
1.				
2.				
3.				
4.				
5.				
Total Team Points				
6.				
7.				

College and University Cross Country Score Sheet

EVENT _____ DATE _____ Site _____ Weather _____

Condition of Course _____ Course Distance _____ Course Record _____

Place	Name	Time	Team
1.			
2.			
3.			
4.			
5.			
6.			
7.			
8.			
9.			
10.			
11.			
12.			
13.			
14.			
15.			
16.			
17.			
18.			
19.			
20.			
21.			
22.			
23.			
24.			
25.			
26.			
27.			
28.			
29.			
30.			
31.			
32.			
33.			
34.			
35.			
36.			
37.			
38.			
39.			
40.			

Place	Name	Time	Team
41.			
42.			
43.			
44.			
45.			
46.			
47.			
48.			
49.			
50.			

Team Results

Team		OA Place	Time	Points
1.				
2.				
3.				
4.				
5.				
Total Team Points				
6.				
7.				

Team		OA Place	Time	Points
1.				
2.				
3.				
4.				
5.				
Total Team Points				
6.				
7.				

College and University Cross Country Score Sheet

EVENT _____ DATE _____ Site _____ Weather _____

Condition of Course _____ Course Distance _____ Course Record _____

Place	Name	Time	Team
1.			
2.			
3.			
4.			
5.			
6.			
7.			
8.			
9.			
10.			
11.			
12.			
13.			
14.			
15.			
16.			
17.			
18.			
19.			
20.			
21.			
22.			
23.			
24.			
25.			
26.			
27.			
28.			
29.			
30.			
31.			
32.			
33.			
34.			
35.			
36.			
37.			
38.			
39.			
40.			

Place	Name	Time	Team
41.			
42.			
43.			
44.			
45.			
46.			
47.			
48.			
49.			
50.			

Team Results

Team		OA Place	Time	Points
1.				
2.				
3.				
4.				
5.				
Total Team Points				
6.				
7.				

Team		OA Place	Time	Points
1.				
2.				
3.				
4.				
5.				
Total Team Points				
6.				
7.				

David Thompson

College and University Cross Country Score Sheet

EVENT _____ **DATE** _____ **Site** _____ **Weather** _____

Condition of Course _____ **Course Distance** _____ **Course Record** _____

Place	Name	Time	Team
1.			
2.			
3.			
4.			
5.			
6.			
7.			
8.			
9.			
10.			
11.			
12.			
13.			
14.			
15.			
16.			
17.			
18.			
19.			
20.			
21.			
22.			
23.			
24.			
25.			
26.			
27.			
28.			
29.			
30.			
31.			
32.			
33.			
34.			
35.			
36.			
37.			
38.			
39.			
40.			

Place	Name	Time	Team
41.			
42.			
43.			
44.			
45.			
46.			
47.			
48.			
49.			
50.			

Team Results

Team		OA Place	Time	Points
1.				
2.				
3.				
4.				
5.				
Total Team Points				
6.				
7.				

Team		OA Place	Time	Points
1.				
2.				
3.				
4.				
5.				
Total Team Points				
6.				
7.				

College and University Cross Country Score Sheet

EVENT _____ DATE _____ Site _____ Weather _____

Condition of Course _____ Course Distance _____ Course Record _____

Place	Name	Time	Team
1.			
2.			
3.			
4.			
5.			
6.			
7.			
8.			
9.			
10.			
11.			
12.			
13.			
14.			
15.			
16.			
17.			
18.			
19.			
20.			
21.			
22.			
23.			
24.			
25.			
26.			
27.			
28.			
29.			
30.			
31.			
32.			
33.			
34.			
35.			
36.			
37.			
38.			
39.			
40.			

Place	Name	Time	Team
41.			
42.			
43.			
44.			
45.			
46.			
47.			
48.			
49.			
50.			

Team Results

Team		OA Place	Time	Points
1.				
2.				
3.				
4.				
5.				
Total Team Points				
6.				
7.				

Team		OA Place	Time	Points
1.				
2.				
3.				
4.				
5.				
Total Team Points				
6.				
7.				

David Thompson

College and University Cross Country Score Sheet

EVENT _____ DATE _____ Site _____ Weather _____

Condition of Course _____ Course Distance _____ Course Record _____

Place	Name	Time	Team
1.			
2.			
3.			
4.			
5.			
6.			
7.			
8.			
9.			
10.			
11.			
12.			
13.			
14.			
15.			
16.			
17.			
18.			
19.			
20.			
21.			
22.			
23.			
24.			
25.			
26.			
27.			
28.			
29.			
30.			
31.			
32.			
33.			
34.			
35.			
36.			
37.			
38.			
39.			
40.			

Place	Name	Time	Team
41.			
42.			
43.			
44.			
45.			
46.			
47.			
48.			
49.			
50.			

Team Results

Team		OA Place	Time	Points
1.				
2.				
3.				
4.				
5.				
Total Team Points				
6.				
7.				

Team		OA Place	Time	Points
1.				
2.				
3.				
4.				
5.				
Total Team Points				
6.				
7.				

College and University Cross Country Score Sheet

EVENT _____ **DATE** _____ **Site** _____ **Weather** _____

Condition of Course _____ **Course Distance** _____ **Course Record** _____

Place	Name	Time	Team
1.			
2.			
3.			
4.			
5.			
6.			
7.			
8.			
9.			
10.			
11.			
12.			
13.			
14.			
15.			
16.			
17.			
18.			
19.			
20.			
21.			
22.			
23.			
24.			
25.			
26.			
27.			
28.			
29.			
30.			
31.			
32.			
33.			
34.			
35.			
36.			
37.			
38.			
39.			
40.			

Place	Name	Time	Team
41.			
42.			
43.			
44.			
45.			
46.			
47.			
48.			
49.			
50.			

Team Results

Team		OA Place	Time	Points
1.				
2.				
3.				
4.				
5.				
Total Team Points				
6.				
7.				

Team		OA Place	Time	Points
1.				
2.				
3.				
4.				
5.				
Total Team Points				
6.				
7.				

College and University Cross Country Score Sheet

EVENT _____ DATE _____ Site _____ Weather _____

Condition of Course _____ Course Distance _____ Course Record _____

Place	Name	Time	Team
1.			
2.			
3.			
4.			
5.			
6.			
7.			
8.			
9.			
10.			
11.			
12.			
13.			
14.			
15.			
16.			
17.			
18.			
19.			
20.			
21.			
22.			
23.			
24.			
25.			
26.			
27.			
28.			
29.			
30.			
31.			
32.			
33.			
34.			
35.			
36.			
37.			
38.			
39.			
40.			

Place	Name	Time	Team
41.			
42.			
43.			
44.			
45.			
46.			
47.			
48.			
49.			
50.			

Team Results

Team		OA Place	Time	Points
1.				
2.				
3.				
4.				
5.				
Total Team Points				
6.				
7.				

Team		OA Place	Time	Points
1.				
2.				
3.				
4.				
5.				
Total Team Points				
6.				
7.				

College and University Cross Country Score Sheet

EVENT _____ **DATE** _____ **Site** _____ **Weather** _____

Condition of Course _____ **Course Distance** _____ **Course Record** _____

Place	Name	Time	Team
1.			
2.			
3.			
4.			
5.			
6.			
7.			
8.			
9.			
10.			
11.			
12.			
13.			
14.			
15.			
16.			
17.			
18.			
19.			
20.			
21.			
22.			
23.			
24.			
25.			
26.			
27.			
28.			
29.			
30.			
31.			
32.			
33.			
34.			
35.			
36.			
37.			
38.			
39.			
40.			

Place	Name	Time	Team
41.			
42.			
43.			
44.			
45.			
46.			
47.			
48.			
49.			
50.			

Team Results

Team		OA Place	Time	Points
1.				
2.				
3.				
4.				
5.				
Total Team Points				
6.				
7.				

Team		OA Place	Time	Points
1.				
2.				
3.				
4.				
5.				
Total Team Points				
6.				
7.				

Indoor Track and Field Season

Indoor Track Attendance Calendar
College and University Indoor Track and Field – Order of Events
Athletes Scoring Sheet
Field Event Scoring Sheet

Indoor Track Attendance Calendar

Month: _____   Coach: _____

Date: _____   Season: _____

Student Name	M	Tu	W	Th	F	Sa	Su	M	Tu	W	Th	F	Sa	Su	M	Tu	W	Th	F	Sa	Su	M	Tu	W	Th	F	Sa	Su	T	U	E	P

Enter: T=Tardy, U=Unexcused, E=Excused , P=Present   Totals

David Thompson

Indoor Track Attendance Calendar

Month: _____   Coach: _____

Date: _____   Season: _____

Student Name	M	Tu	W	Th	F	Sa	Su	M	Tu	W	Th	F	Sa	Su	M	Tu	W	Th	F	Sa	Su	M	Tu	W	Th	F	Sa	Su	T	U	E	P

Enter: T=Tardy, U=Unexcused, E=Excused, P=Present — Totals

74

Indoor Track Attendance Calendar

Month: _____   Coach: _____

Date: _____   Season: _____

	Enter: T=Tardy, U=Unexcused, E=Excused , P=Present																												Totals			
Student Name	M	Tu	W	Th	F	Sa	Su	M	Tu	W	Th	F	Sa	Su	M	Tu	W	Th	F	Sa	Su	M	Tu	W	Th	F	Sa	Su	T	U	E	P

Indoor Track Attendance Calendar

Month: _____   Coach: _____

Date: _____   Season: _____

Student Name	Enter: T=Tardy, U=Unexcused, E=Excused , P=Present																												Totals			
	M	Tu	W	Th	F	Sa	Su	M	Tu	W	Th	F	Sa	Su	M	Tu	W	Th	F	Sa	Su	M	Tu	W	Th	F	Sa	Su	T	U	E	P

Indoor Track Attendance Calendar

Month: _____   Coach: _____

Date: _____   Season: _____

Student Name	Enter: T=Tardy, U=Unexcused, E=Excused , P=Present																												Totals			
	M	Tu	W	Th	F	Sa	Su	M	Tu	W	Th	F	Sa	Su	M	Tu	W	Th	F	Sa	Su	M	Tu	W	Th	F	Sa	Su	T	U	E	P

Indoor Track Attendance Calendar

Month: _____   Coach: _____

Date: _____   Season: _____

Student Name	M	Tu	W	Th	F	Sa	Su	M	Tu	W	Th	F	Sa	Su	M	Tu	W	Th	F	Sa	Su	M	Tu	W	Th	F	Sa	Su	T	U	E	P

Enter: T=Tardy, U=Unexcused, E=Excused , P=Present — Totals

College and University Indoor Track and Field – Order of Events

Scoring Results Points

Men/Women _____ / _____

Date: _____

1st place 5pts 2nd place 3pts 3rd place 1pt 5pts 4 x 400m/4 x 100m					
Events	**First**	**Second**	**Third**	**Home**	**Visitor**
Long Jump					
Triple Jump					
Pole Vault					
Shot put					
High Jump					
5000m					
3000m					
60m Hurdle Trials					
60m Dash Trials					
1000m					
600m					
4 x 200m					
1 mile					
60m Hurdle Finals					
60m Dash Finals					
800m run					
400m					
200m					
4 x 800m Relay					
4 x 400m Relay					
4 x 1600m					
Final score					

College and University Indoor Track and Field – Order of Events

Scoring Results Points

Men/Women _____ / _____

Date: _____

1st place 5pts 2nd place 3pts 3rd place 1pt 5pts 4x400m/4x100m					
Events	First	Second	Third	Home	Visitor
Long Jump					
Triple Jump					
Pole Vault					
Shot put					
High Jump					
5000m					
3000m					
60m Hurdle Trials					
60m Dash Trials					
1000m					
600m					
4x 200m					
1 mile					
60m Hurdle Finals					
60m Dash Finals					
800m run					
400m					
200m					
4x 800m Relay					
4x 400m Relay					
4x 1600m					
Final score					

College and University Indoor Track and Field – Order of Events

Scoring Results Points

Men/Women _____ / _____

Date: _____

1st place 5pts 2nd place 3pts 3rd place 1pt 5pts 4x400m/4x100m					
Events	**First**	**Second**	**Third**	**Home**	**Visitor**
Long Jump					
Triple Jump					
Pole Vault					
Shot put					
High Jump					
5000m					
3000m					
60m Hurdle Trials					
60m Dash Trials					
1000m					
600m					
4x200m					
1 mile					
60m Hurdle Finals					
60m Dash Finals					
800m run					
400m					
200m					
4x800m Relay					
4x400m Relay					
4x1600m					
Final score					

David Thompson

College and University Indoor Track and Field – Order of Events

Scoring Results Points

Men/Women _____ / _____

Date: _____

1st place 5pts 2nd place 3pts 3rd place 1pt 5pts 4x400m/4x100m					
Events	**First**	**Second**	**Third**	**Home**	**Visitor**
Long Jump					
Triple Jump					
Pole Vault					
Shot put					
High Jump					
5000m					
3000m					
60m Hurdle Trials					
60m Dash Trials					
1000m					
600m					
4x 200m					
1 mile					
60m Hurdle Finals					
60m Dash Finals					
800m run					
400m					
200m					
4x 800m Relay					
4x 400m Relay					
4x 1600m					
Final score					

College and University Indoor Track and Field – Order of Events

Scoring Results Points

Men/Women _____ / _____

Date: _____

1ˢᵗ place 5pts 2ⁿᵈ place 3pts 3ʳᵈ place 1pt 5pts 4 x 400m/4 x 100m					
Events	**First**	**Second**	**Third**	**Home**	**Visitor**
Long Jump					
Triple Jump					
Pole Vault					
Shot put					
High Jump					
5000m					
3000m					
60m Hurdle Trials					
60m Dash Trials					
1000m					
600m					
4 x 200m					
1 mile					
60m Hurdle Finals					
60m Dash Finals					
800m run					
400m					
200m					
4 x 800m Relay					
4 x 400m Relay					
4 x 1600m					
Final score					

David Thompson

College and University Indoor Track and Field – Order of Events

Scoring Results Points

Men/Women _____ / _____

Date: _____

1ˢᵗ place 5pts 2ⁿᵈ place 3pts 3ʳᵈ place 1pt 5pts 4×400m/4×100m					
Events	First	Second	Third	Home	Visitor
Long Jump					
Triple Jump					
Pole Vault					
Shot put					
High Jump					
5000m					
3000m					
60m Hurdle Trials					
60m Dash Trials					
1000m					
600m					
4x 200m					
1 mile					
60m Hurdle Finals					
60m Dash Finals					
800m run					
400m					
200m					
4x 800m Relay					
4x 400m Relay					
4x 1600m					
Final score					

College and University Indoor Track and Field - Order of Events

Scoring Results Points

Men/Women _____ / _____

Date: _____

1st place 5pts 2nd place 3pts 3rd place 1pt 5pts 4x400m/4x100m					
Events	**First**	**Second**	**Third**	**Home**	**Visitor**
Long Jump					
Triple Jump					
Pole Vault					
Shot put					
High Jump					
5000m					
3000m					
60m Hurdle Trials					
60m Dash Trials					
1000m					
600m					
4 x 200m					
1 mile					
60m Hurdle Finals					
60m Dash Finals					
800m run					
400m					
200m					
4 x 800m Relay					
4 x 400m Relay					
4 x 1600m					
Final score					

College and University Indoor Track and Field – Order of Events

Scoring Results Points

Men/Women _____ / _____

Date: _____

1st place 5pts 2nd place 3pts 3rd place 1pt 5pts 4x400m/4x100m					
Events	First	Second	Third	Home	Visitor
Long Jump					
Triple Jump					
Pole Vault					
Shot put					
High Jump					
5000m					
3000m					
60m Hurdle Trials					
60m Dash Trials					
1000m					
600m					
4x 200m					
1 mile					
60m Hurdle Finals					
60m Dash Finals					
800m run					
400m					
200m					
4x 800m Relay					
4x 400m Relay					
4x 1600m					
Final score					

College and University Indoor Track and Field – Order of Events

Scoring Results Points

Men/Women _____ / _____

Date: _____

1st place 5pts 2nd place 3pts 3rd place 1pt 5pts 4x400m/4x100m					
Events	**First**	**Second**	**Third**	**Home**	**Visitor**
Long Jump					
Triple Jump					
Pole Vault					
Shot put					
High Jump					
5000m					
3000m					
60m Hurdle Trials					
60m Dash Trials					
1000m					
600m					
4 x 200m					
1 mile					
60m Hurdle Finals					
60m Dash Finals					
800m run					
400m					
200m					
4 x 800m Relay					
4 x 400m Relay					
4 x 1600m					
Final score					

David Thompson

College and University Indoor Track and Field – Order of Events

Scoring Results Points

Men/Women _____ / _____

Date: _____

1st place 5pts 2nd place 3pts 3rd place 1pt 5pts 4x400m/4x100m					
Events	**First**	**Second**	**Third**	**Home**	**Visitor**
Long Jump					
Triple Jump					
Pole Vault					
Shot put					
High Jump					
5000m					
3000m					
60m Hurdle Trials					
60m Dash Trials					
1000m					
600m					
4x 200m					
1 mile					
60m Hurdle Finals					
60m Dash Finals					
800m run					
400m					
200m					
4x 800m Relay					
4x 400m Relay					
4x 1600m					
Final score					

Athletes Scoring Sheet

Name	Event	Results
1.		
2.		
3.		
4.		
5.		
6.		
7.		
8.		
9.		
10.		
11.		
12.		
13.		
14.		
15.		
16.		
17.		
18.		
19.		
20.		
21.		
22.		
23.		
24.		
25.		
26.		
27.		
28.		
29.		
30.		

David Thompson

Athletes Scoring Sheet

Name	Event	Results
1.		
2.		
3.		
4.		
5.		
6.		
7.		
8.		
9.		
10.		
11.		
12.		
13.		
14.		
15.		
16.		
17.		
18.		
19.		
20.		
21.		
22.		
23.		
24.		
25.		
26.		
27.		
28.		
29.		
30.		

Athletes Scoring Sheet

Name	Event	Results
1.		
2.		
3.		
4.		
5.		
6.		
7.		
8.		
9.		
10.		
11.		
12.		
13.		
14.		
15.		
16.		
17.		
18.		
19.		
20.		
21.		
22.		
23.		
24.		
25.		
26.		
27.		
28.		
29.		
30.		

Athletes Scoring Sheet

Name	Event	Results
1.		
2.		
3.		
4.		
5.		
6.		
7.		
8.		
9.		
10.		
11.		
12.		
13.		
14.		
15.		
16.		
17.		
18.		
19.		
20.		
21.		
22.		
23.		
24.		
25.		
26.		
27.		
28.		
29.		
30.		

Athletes Scoring Sheet

Name	Event	Results
1.		
2.		
3.		
4.		
5.		
6.		
7.		
8.		
9.		
10.		
11.		
12.		
13.		
14.		
15.		
16.		
17.		
18.		
19.		
20.		
21.		
22.		
23.		
24.		
25.		
26.		
27.		
28.		
29.		
30.		

Athletes Scoring Sheet

Name	Event	Results
1.		
2.		
3.		
4.		
5.		
6.		
7.		
8.		
9.		
10.		
11.		
12.		
13.		
14.		
15.		
16.		
17.		
18.		
19.		
20.		
21.		
22.		
23.		
24.		
25.		
26.		
27.		
28.		
29.		
30.		

Athletes Scoring Sheet

Name	Event	Results
1.		
2.		
3.		
4.		
5.		
6.		
7.		
8.		
9.		
10.		
11.		
12.		
13.		
14.		
15.		
16.		
17.		
18.		
19.		
20.		
21.		
22.		
23.		
24.		
25.		
26.		
27.		
28.		
29.		
30.		

David Thompson

Athletes Scoring Sheet

Name	Event	Results
1.		
2.		
3.		
4.		
5.		
6.		
7.		
8.		
9.		
10.		
11.		
12.		
13.		
14.		
15.		
16.		
17.		
18.		
19.		
20.		
21.		
22.		
23.		
24.		
25.		
26.		
27.		
28.		
29.		
30.		

Athletes Scoring Sheet

Name	Event	Results
1.		
2.		
3.		
4.		
5.		
6.		
7.		
8.		
9.		
10.		
11.		
12.		
13.		
14.		
15.		
16.		
17.		
18.		
19.		
20.		
21.		
22.		
23.		
24.		
25.		
26.		
27.		
28.		
29.		
30.		

Athletes Scoring Sheet

Name	Event	Results
1.		
2.		
3.		
4.		
5.		
6.		
7.		
8.		
9.		
10.		
11.		
12.		
13.		
14.		
15.		
16.		
17.		
18.		
19.		
20.		
21.		
22.		
23.		
24.		
25.		
26.		
27.		
28.		
29.		
30.		

Field Event Scoring Sheet

Men/Women: _____ Date: _____ .

Long Jump/ Hammer	Triple Jump	Shot Put	Discus	Javelin	High Jump	Pole Vault
Name	School	1ˢᵗ Attempt	2ⁿᵈ Attempt	3ʳᵈ Attempt	Best	Place
1.						
2.						
3.						
4.						
5.						
6.						
7.						
8.						
9.						
10.						
11.						
12.						
13.						
14.						
15.						
16.						
17.						
18.						
19.						
20.						
21.						
22.						
23.						
24.						
25.						
26.						
27.						
28.						
29.						
30.						

Field Event Scoring Sheet

Men/Women: _____ Date: _____ .

Long Jump/ Hammer	Triple Jump	Shot Put	Discus	Javelin	High Jump	Pole Vault
Name	School	1ˢᵗ Attempt	2ⁿᵈ Attempt	3ʳᵈ Attempt	Best	Place
1.						
2.						
3.						
4.						
5.						
6.						
7.						
8.						
9.						
10.						
11.						
12.						
13.						
14.						
15.						
16.						
17.						
18.						
19.						
20.						
21.						
22.						
23.						
24.						
25.						
26.						
27.						
28.						
29.						
30.						

Field Event Scoring Sheet

Men/Women: _____   Date: _____ .

Long Jump/ Hammer	Triple Jump	Shot Put	Discus	Javelin	High Jump	Pole Vault
Name	School	1ˢᵗ Attempt	2ⁿᵈ Attempt	3ʳᵈ Attempt	Best	Place
1.						
2.						
3.						
4.						
5.						
6.						
7.						
8.						
9.						
10.						
11.						
12.						
13.						
14.						
15.						
16.						
17.						
18.						
19.						
20.						
21.						
22.						
23.						
24.						
25.						
26.						
27.						
28.						
29.						
30.						

David Thompson

Field Event Scoring Sheet

Men/Women: _____ Date: _____ .

Long Jump/ Hammer	Triple Jump	Shot Put	Discus	Javelin	High Jump	Pole Vault
Name	School	1ˢᵗ Attempt	2ⁿᵈ Attempt	3ʳᵈ Attempt	Best	Place
1.						
2.						
3.						
4.						
5.						
6.						
7.						
8.						
9.						
10.						
11.						
12.						
13.						
14.						
15.						
16.						
17.						
18.						
19.						
20.						
21.						
22.						
23.						
24.						
25.						
26.						
27.						
28.						
29.						
30.						

Field Event Scoring Sheet

Men/Women: _____ Date: _____ .

Long Jump/ Hammer	Triple Jump	Shot Put	Discus	Javelin	High Jump	Pole Vault
Name	School	1ˢᵗ Attempt	2ⁿᵈ Attempt	3ʳᵈ Attempt	Best	Place
1.						
2.						
3.						
4.						
5.						
6.						
7.						
8.						
9.						
10.						
11.						
12.						
13.						
14.						
15.						
16.						
17.						
18.						
19.						
20.						
21.						
22.						
23.						
24.						
25.						
26.						
27.						
28.						
29.						
30.						

Field Event Scoring Sheet

Men/Women: _____ Date: _____ .

Long Jump/ Hammer	Triple Jump	Shot Put	Discus	Javelin	High Jump	Pole Vault
Name	School	1st Attempt	2nd Attempt	3rd Attempt	Best	Place
1.						
2.						
3.						
4.						
5.						
6.						
7.						
8.						
9.						
10.						
11.						
12.						
13.						
14.						
15.						
16.						
17.						
18.						
19.						
20.						
21.						
22.						
23.						
24.						
25.						
26.						
27.						
28.						
29.						
30.						

Field Event Scoring Sheet

Men/Women: _____ Date: _____ .

Long Jump/ Hammer	Triple Jump	Shot Put	Discus	Javelin	High Jump	Pole Vault
Name	School	1ᵗ Attempt	2ⁿᵈ Attempt	3ʳᵈ Attempt	Best	Place
1.						
2.						
3.						
4.						
5.						
6.						
7.						
8.						
9.						
10.						
11.						
12.						
13.						
14.						
15.						
16.						
17.						
18.						
19.						
20.						
21.						
22.						
23.						
24.						
25.						
26.						
27.						
28.						
29.						
30.						

Field Event Scoring Sheet

Men/Women: _____ Date: _____ .

Long Jump/ Hammer	Triple Jump	Shot Put	Discus	Javelin	High Jump	Pole Vault
Name	School	1ˢᵗ Attempt	2ⁿᵈ Attempt	3ʳᵈ Attempt	Best	Place
1.						
2.						
3.						
4.						
5.						
6.						
7.						
8.						
9.						
10.						
11.						
12.						
13.						
14.						
15.						
16.						
17.						
18.						
19.						
20.						
21.						
22.						
23.						
24.						
25.						
26.						
27.						
28.						
29.						
30.						

Field Event Scoring Sheet

Men/Women: _____ Date: _____ .

Long Jump/ Hammer	Triple Jump	Shot Put	Discus	Javelin	High Jump	Pole Vault
Name	School	1ˢᵗ Attempt	2ⁿᵈ Attempt	3ʳᵈ Attempt	Best	Place
1.						
2.						
3.						
4.						
5.						
6.						
7.						
8.						
9.						
10.						
11.						
12.						
13.						
14.						
15.						
16.						
17.						
18.						
19.						
20.						
21.						
22.						
23.						
24.						
25.						
26.						
27.						
28.						
29.						
30.						

David Thompson

Field Event Scoring Sheet

Men/Women: _____ Date: _____ .

Long Jump/ Hammer	Triple Jump	Shot Put	Discus	Javelin	High Jump	Pole Vault
Name	**School**	**1ˢᵗ Attempt**	**2ⁿᵈ Attempt**	**3ʳᵈ Attempt**	**Best**	**Place**
1.						
2.						
3.						
4.						
5.						
6.						
7.						
8.						
9.						
10.						
11.						
12.						
13.						
14.						
15.						
16.						
17.						
18.						
19.						
20.						
21.						
22.						
23.						
24.						
25.						
26.						
27.						
28.						
29.						
30.						

Coach Survey

Underneath are a few questions pertaining to a coach's rating. This would require you to give out a rating for the coach on a five-point scale. If the query or situation stated does not apply to you, please feel free to leave it blank. Alternatively, you can also give an answer that is closest possible to your experience for improving the results of the study.

5 = Beyond Expectations	4 = Impressive	3= Decent	2 = Needs To Improve	1=Fail				
Coach Survey					1	2	3	4	5
The coach seemingly possesses sufficient knowledge pertaining to conditioning									
The coach is capable of communicating that knowledge to their students									
The coach has a sufficient amount of experience and knowledge to justifiably judge talent									
The coach's call is wise and fair, even in the eyes of the supporters									
After a game, the coach always appreciates and rewards a good performance, but also highlights the points of improvement that can help his students get better									
The coach manages to organize regular practice sessions to keep their students									
The coach emphasizes on conducting regular drills									
The coach extends valuable criticisms and wise suggestions									
The coach tends to recognize the importance of maximum encouragements and criticism									
The coach can be seen appreciating conditioning									
The coach teaches individual techniques and skills quite well									
The coach encourages good team work									
The coach tends to make practice look fun									
The coach commands the respect of every person on the field during practice									
The coach takes responsibility for the health and safety of the student									
The coach efficiently utilizes every session of practice									
The coach is approachable to students									
The coach always presents a game in both the individual and team aspects									
The coach has the ability to motivate their students									
The coach is calm, cool and collective instead of being impatient									

David Thompson

5 = Beyond Expectations	4 = Impressive	3= Decent	2 = Needs To Improve	1=Fail				
Coach Survey					1	2	3	4	5
The coach regularly communicates their opinions and suggestions to the student.									
The coach uses no foul language, as doing so would be unacceptable.									
The coach needs the student-athlete to perform up to team expectations.									
The coach imparts a sufficient amount of attention to each student.									
The coach motivates the team even after being defeated by the competition.									
The coach seems trustworthy.									
The coach is a likable person.									
The coach commands the respect of the team.									
The coach is interested in me as a person.									
The coach appreciates all the student-athletes and motivates them.									
At a student meeting, the coach gives everyone a fair chance to state their opinions and working out alternatives. Does the coach listen to the student?									
The coach conducts themselves in an orderly fashion pertaining to the students									
The coach's targets set for their student-athletes are achievable.									
The coach has sufficient knowledge of discipline; as well as when and when not to use it.									
The coach tends to take their student goals as their own and assist the student throughout.									
The coach proves to be dedicated to maintaining the standards and conduct of the sport.									

5 = Beyond Expectations	4 = Impressive	3= Decent	2 = Needs To Improve	1=Fail				
Coach Survey					1	2	3	4	5
The coach dresses exemplarily for all meetings and dinners.									
The coach's outlook serves as a good role model for their students.									
The coach can appreciate a good joke from time to time.									
The coach serves as the role model and the frontline for the team during any and all competition.									
The coach conducts themselves in an orderly fashion especially when addressing any of the officials at any given competitions.									
The coach bucks students to indulge in social activities.									
The coach shows interest in the career choices and work of all their students.									
The coach proves possession of relevant knowledge pertaining to the sport and the many strategies therein.									
The coach is as much a part of practice as the student.									
The coach ensures the students are physically and mentally ready to deal with each step of every competition.									
The coach doesn't abuse or demean the students they manage and coach.									
This coach doesn't abuse their students.									
The coach is easy to talk to and helps out wherever they can.									
The coach shows sufficient concern regarding the student as a whole person and not just the athlete part of the student.									

David Thompson

We extend our warmest thanks to you, for enriching this experience with your contribution to this season. Please take a couple minutes to state your opinions about this season; your take on the matter, if you will. For example, what you think worked or didn't work well, what we should or shouldn't change etc.

Please do convey your suggestions if you have any; be they regarding strategies or techniques that you may want to see.

Thank you once again.

COMMENTS:_____
_____
_____
_____
_____
_____
_____
_____
_____
_____
_____
_____
_____
_____
_____
_____
_____
_____
_____
_____

Ten Commandments for The Runner

1. Thou shalt not compare thyself to thy fellow runners. A mile art a mile.
2. Thou shalt exclaimeth naught that "I art not a runner." If thou runneth, thou art a runner.
3. Thou shalt not leave thine slumber.
4. Remembereth thine "day of respite" and keepeth that day holiest.
5. Honor thine muscles and thine "aches and pains" and push naught through injury. As a Runner thou art strong but naught invincible.
6. Thou shalt remember to water thine body and thank thy lord for such bounteous blessings.
7. Thou shalt not the sin by adorning thineself with garments of cotton, for it doth naught favor thou (especially on the glorious day of the race).
8. Thou shalt not ignore thine shoes, shineth them for they be tools of an artist painting a picture. Taketh pride in thine tools.
9. Thou shalt get stuck in a "rut," nevermore, for thou shalt rely on variance in thine running by way of ascention, destination, and thine swiftness.
10. Thou shalt never covet thy neighbor's medals or money (Or cars thou art a runner after all.)

Athletes' Prayers

Dearest of all, my Lord,
In this ongoing battle we have through life,
I ask for nothing more; than a field which may be fair,
A grounding that is equal beside everyone else,
A strength unmatched to persevere and a heart that dares to dare.
For if, perchance, I shall win, I want it to be fair,
With my Faith and Head held high.
For it is your glory that would have gotten me by,
But if I should lose, let me stand strong,
stand alone, beside the road
And cheer gloriously as our champions pass by.

I run because I can

I run for it is a blessing that I can When I get weary and worn out
I recall all those who cannot partake in a good run.
What wouldn't they give to be blessed with this simple
unappreciated gift? A gift that I have taken for granted
And so I began to run harder, stronger and faster, for then I run for them.
Because I know they would, and then they would have done some more for me.

I'm a Runner!

I run on frozen rivers…I sprint through scorching sun,
I run among the tied trails of destiny …I run openly freely in the streets,
In days that are good and all the same in the days that are bad …I run
through it all, through the anguish through all the pains,
Be it Snow…sleet… even in the toughest rains,
Alone with my thoughts or racing against the field,
I have no choice, never to stop never to yield,
"It's WHO I AM and That's The Runner's Way"

Runner's Prayer

Run beside me.
Live in my heart's every beat.
Give me strength, as this cold surrounds me.
As the wind pushes me back now.
I know I'm surrounded by you.
As this relentless sun will warm me, as these harsh rains will cleanse.
I know you are on me I can feel you clinging to my skin.
Challenging me, provoking me, loving me and teaching me,
So I forever gave in to this run.
Thank you for matching my every stride since day one.
Amen

The Athlete's Prayer

O Lord, please cleanse my mind of all my worries and my heart of all its burdens.
So, I may glorify your name, glorify it with victory.
Knowing beside me here, you'll always be, ever-close to me.
Please raise me before that moment strikes, so I may see, and better understand your glory.
Every time I walk upon this field every time this game unfolds in front of me.

With great courage I will meet this challenge, as you would have me to.
But my heart please keep humble and in remembrance of mine keep;
All this glory, my strength and success they come directly from you-the ever giving.
Then when I walk in front of those eyes, when they all rest upon me, when the dust it has
settled and the champions have been declared. I will turn them onto the path of you,
My Lord, and to your name they too shall bring glory.
Amen

Coach's Prayer

O' Lord God, grant me insight; from which to see the thine glory in
all; patience to strengthen those you bestow upon me,
Betterment; and the mind to at all times be a winning example. May those I
teach forever see you in me and become closer to you; through me.
With your Graceful name, I pray Glory forever be to your name.
Amen

When I run

Whenever I run, I pray not to win, not to vanquish my foes. But to glorify the
name of God using all the talents the Almighty has blessed me with.
I pray to keep intact my integrity & character. Always shall
they be a representation of my lord and savior.

I am a long-distance runner

I am a runner of magnanimous-distances. I keep going even when it's hard as I have been trained.
Even when it hurts. Even when it breaks. Even when I can't. I look beyond it.
Relentlessly my war to the finish wages. Call it whatever you may desire to: obduracy,
survival, idiocy, stubbornness, rebellion, resolve, determination or moral fiber.
But deep down I know it's much simpler than this; I just can't give up.
(And it's always worth it in the end.)

Why Is Sleep a Priority in Any Athlete's Training Schedule

As recently as 2008, we witnessed Usain Bolt breaking records at the Beijing Olympics. He became the first man in history who holds a world record for his 100m and 200m dashes. By 2012, he was known as a force to be reckoned with when he broke another record. This was for being the first man in history to secure 6 Olympic gold medals.

So, what does this 6-time Olympic gold standard sprinter consider as the most important part of his training? The answer is sleep. This may seem simple but you will feel unbeatable after a good night's rest. Mr. Bolt's statement regarding the issue was:

"Sleep is extremely important to me – I need to rest and recover in order for the training I do to be absorbed by my body" – Usain Bolt.

As the experts, we cannot begin to explain the importance of sleep. It's highly essential for an athlete since it is required for muscle growth and sustenance. Pro-sports teams like, the Vancouver Canucks ensure that there is just the perfect amount of sleep in each athlete's schedule. This is done to ensure maximum growth in each player.

Key Infographic Takeaways

  • By incorporating an appropriate amount of sleep into their routines, athletes gain a 42% boost in accuracy

  • Sleep tends to improve instantaneous critical decision-making ability by a whopping 4.3%

  • After withstanding sleep deprivation for 4 days, athletes tend to slip off the edge; power house athletes lose a maximum bench press by as much as 20lbs

  • Roger Federer puts in 11 to 12 hours of sleep every night, ensuring his body rests just as hard as he plays.

  • Lebron James gets 12 hours of sleep per night ensuring accuracy; brilliance can tire a body so cool down before your barrel melts, young gun

Why More Sleep May Improve Sports Performance

Researchers have speculated that extended deep sleep tends to improve athletic performance. This is the time when the maximum amounts of growth hormones are released. These specific growth hormones look after muscle growth and repair. They even expedite athlete recovery.

How Much Sleep Do You Need?

Experts say that 20 hours of sleep deprivation adversely affect you. Athletes tend to have lesser tolerance for disruptions like this in their schedules.

Sleep experts recommend seven to nine hours of daily sleep for adults, and nine to ten hours for adolescents and teens. You could experiment over a few weeks and figure it out.

The test is simple, if you fall asleep within 20 minutes and wake up at a predetermined time, you're good. Chances are that you are probably getting the perfect amount of sleep and waking up fresh as berry every day. If not, you need help fixing your sleep routine.

Most recreational athletes have stated that "a sleepless night" once in a while does not adversely affect your performance.

How to Use Sleep to Improve Sports Performance

- Mark it as a priority in your schedule

- Increase your sleep, weeks before a competition

- Sleep and wake up at a fixed time

- Take naps to compensate for lost sleep

Appendix A: Diet and Nutrition for Track and Field Athletes

One of the most important jobs you have as a track and field runner is taking responsibility for your diet and nutrition. Your body is a high-performance machine, and it needs the right fuel to keep it running fast and steady—and to ensure overall good health.

When to eat

Listen to your own body and trust it to know how often you should eat. Don't allow yourself to get overfull, but don't deprive yourself either. Look for the balance that is right for you, eating no less than four meals a day and no more than six. Don't skip breakfast. It's the most important meal of the day and comes after your body has been without an energy source for about 10 to 12 hours. Feel free to have healthy snacks in between meals, staying away from snacks that are loaded with sugar.

Hydration is also key for runners. Exercise makes you hot, and then you sweat as your body tries to cool itself down. That water must be replaced. Drink at least 64 ounces of water each day, and make sure you make extra efforts to hydrate before a meet and rehydrate afterwards.

What to eat

Again, balance is the key. You'll want to eat a combination of carbohydrates—or carbs—which provide fuel for the muscle groups you rely on as an athlete; proteins to build and repair muscle tissue and even out your metabolism; and fats that provide endurance and sustained energy. Stay away from foods that are loaded with preservatives or foods that are engineered or genetically modified. Shop the perimeter of the grocery store, where you'll find meats, fruits and vegetables, and dairy products—real foods prepared without preservatives. Look for labels that say, "Non-GMO," meaning they are not genetically modified.

Suggested foods and food groups

- Eggs are a great source of protein. One egg provides 10 percent of your daily protein needs as well as amino acids that promote muscle recovery, vitamin K, and a nutrient that aids in brain health. Eggs were once associated with high cholesterol and heart disease, but recent studies refute those claims. Eat eggs eagerly. Since you're likely a busy person balancing athletics with academics, boil a dozen eggs at a time to have them ready as a grab-and-go food.

- Whole-grain cereal, bread, and pasta are good sources of fiber, carbs, and protein. Stay away from cereals that are loaded with sugar and search instead for cereals that are high in fiber. Stay away from the empty calories in white bread and pasta too; whole grains give you a lot morepower and energy. Remember that you can sprinkle cereal on yogurt and salad as well as relying on it as a meal.

- Yogurt is a good source of protein and calcium, and Greek yogurts that are popular today are
- tasty and also contain live cultures that benefit the digestive tract.

- Nuts such as almonds, walnuts, and cashews are also a source for vitamins and minerals and are known to lower the risk for heart disease. While they are also a great source for protein, they are also high in calories, so eat them in moderation. You can sprinkle nuts on salads, pasta dishes, or yogurt; make a trail mix with dried fruits—and maybe some pieces of chocolate to reward you—; or enjoy them on their own in a one-ounce serving dish.

- Fruits and vegetables are excellent sources of vitamins and minerals. Oranges in particular are a great food source, rich in Vitamin C, of course, which can help alleviate muscle pain, and it's also loaded with antioxidants. Fruits like oranges, apples, bananas, and grapes are also easy foods to eat on the run. They make good supplements to a meal or can serve as a snack.

- Black beans are a good vegetarian source of protein, fiber, and vitamin B, and you can buy them cooked in a can. Carbs in beans are released slowly over time, which provides you with a nice, steady supply of energy. Black beans are a hearty base for soups, and they can be tossed on salads or blended with chicken in chili.

- Mixed salad greens are popular these days. Blends of greens that include such favorites as radicchio, endive, and romaine offer you nutrients and antioxidants that protect your muscles against damage. Add vegetables such as cucumber, carrots, and celery or go with greens only.
- Salmon, tuna, chicken, and turkey are excellent protein sources and are recommended for lunch as well as dinner. Salmon has omega-3 fats that that helps balance inflammation in the body and ward off various diseases. Because tuna contains mercury, don't eat it every day! Chicken also has Vitamin B that helps regulate fat-burning. Turkey has iron, zinc, and potassium.

Meal suggestions

Breakfast
- Eggs, any way you like them—fried, scrambled, poached, or hard boiled. Add cheese or vegetables to scrambled eggs for additional protein and vitamins.
- Whole-grain oatmeal. Add some fruit!
- Nuts and berries on top of your favorite yogurt.

Lunch
- Chicken, turkey, or tuna with greens and a slice of cheese between two slices of whole-grain bread.
- A mixed green salad with chicken or black beans on the top. Be adventurous and add vegetables! Or sprinkle some hard-boiled egg on top.

Dinner
- Salmon, chicken, or turkey with roasted potatoes or whole-grain rice and lots of vegetables—steamed, roasted, or raw.
- Soups made with beans or lean meats and vegetables. (Stay away from soups made with storebought bouillons as they likely contain more salt than you need.) **Snacks**

Granola bars, fruits, nuts, yogurts, smoothies, trail mix.

Appendix B: History of Track and Field and Cross-country

Track and field as we know it today is a sport that involves running, jumping, and throwing. Cross-country running is a sport in which teams and individuals compete on outdoor courses that take them through fields, woods, and across other rugged terrain in all weather conditions.

While many cross-country competitors also run distance events in track and field, the two sports are separate and distinct. Both fall under the umbrella of "athletics," and events are governed by the International Association of Athletics Federations.

History of Track and Field

Track and field has evolved over time and is believed to be the first and only athletic event of the early Olympic Games. Sources are mixed on when track and field began—perhaps as long ago as the ninth or tenth century BC but certainly by 776 BC. During these games, a cook won a 600-foot race, and some say that event marked the first track and field event.

Sprinting was the only event of the Olympic games in its first 13 festivals, spanning 52 years. The games were held in Olympia every four years and additional sports were added over time. By the fifth century BC, the festival was held over five days and included foot races, a long jump, and throwing events such as discus and javelin.

Track and field came to England during the nineteenth century. Students of public schools and universities held meets—or "meetings," as they are still called in Britain. The first organized track and field meet of modern times was held in 1849 by the Royal Military Academy at Sand Hurst. By that time, running competitions had also developed in the United States and were second in popularity as a spectator sport only to horse racing. Races could draw crowds of 30,000 spectators, and prizes were as much as $1,000. Prized runners, such as George Seward, an early American standout, began to tour the country, competing. Seward toured 23 states and Canada.

Lon Myers was another great American track and field performer. In the 1880s, he beat all competitors from Britain and created world records in America and Britain. His participation is said to have validated track and field in this country.

Around the 1860s, associations formed in the United States to oversee track and field events, and, again, there is some disagreement on which group led the first competition. Those cited as existing from the late 1800s through the early 1900s are the Intercollegiate Association of Amateur Athletes of America, the Amateur Athletic Union of the United States, and the National Association of Amateur Athletes of America. What's significant about these groups is that they elevated the events from those held on horse tracks to those raced on tracks specifically built for the sport. Today—and since 1912—the International Association of Athletics Federations (IAAF) governs professional track and field events across the world.

Track and field experienced a major revival on April 6, 1896, when the Olympic Games were reborn in Athens after being banned by Roman Emperor Theodosius I nearly 1,500 years prior. At the opening of these Athens Games, athletes from 13 nations were welcomed by King Georgios I and a crowd of 60,000 spectators. The Olympics grew steadily in scope and popularity afterwards, and track and field events have been the centerpiece ever since.

As track and field developed as a modern sport, amateur athletes were those who did not accept money or cash prizes, and that was a major issue that sometimes saw top performers stripped of awards. If charged with "professionalism," athletes were banned from competition for life. In 1913, Olympic medals for wins the year before in decathlon and penthalon were taken from Jim Thorpe, an American, after it was learned he had played semi-professional baseball. The awards were restored in 1982, posthumously, by the International Olympic Committee.

Women's participation in track and field began around 1921, when representatives from six countries formed an athletic federation for women, which merged with the IAAF in 1936. The numbers of female athletes in the sport has increased rapidly since then, and in 1928, women's track and field became part of the Olympic Games.

Now in its second century, IAAF aims to continue to inspire athletes of all ages to run, jump, and throw, and to increase audiences. It works to ensure that every facet of the sport is reviewed, tested, and encouraged.

History of Cross-country

Cross-country has its roots in hunting in England in the early 1800s. Runners imitating their sportshunting fathers were designated as either "hares" or "hounds," and chased one another through the woods, leaving a trail of shredded paper. The game was called "Hare and Hounds" or "The Paper Chase."

The younger runners, young teens, made up "the pack," and the hares were older students up to age 18. They ran through the woods with no official course. They forged the trail, crossing streams, climbing hills, and enjoying the "hunt." Shrewsbury School in England is said to be the first school to offer an organized version of the sport, and their hounds were given dog names common at the time, such as "Trojan" or "Challenger." They were to follow the tracks of the more skilled hares, who zigzagged and laid false trails to keep the competition interesting.

In 1837, the first official paper chase was held at Rugby School. Called the Crick Run, it was soon duplicated by other public schools and Oxford and Cambridge universities. Eventually, the game became what we know as the cross-country race. The first national championship was held in England in 1876, and two years later, the sport was introduced in the United States, in New York, by William C. Vosburgh.

Cross-country running was introduced at Harvard in 1880 as a training event for track and field runners, and not long after, the sport became adopted by other colleges and universities; the first intercollegiate meet was held in 1890. a governing association was founded in 1898 with a special assist by Cornell University, where the sport was particularly popular.

International cross-country racing also began in 1898 with competition between England and France. England became involved in an annual competition with Ireland, Scotland, and Wales in 1903, and in 1907, France joined in, as did additional European nations in the 1920s.

Cross-country was on the Olympic program three times between 1912 and 1924, but it was later considered unsuitable for summer competition and was dropped.

The International Amateur Athletic Federation (IAAF) began to oversee cross-country in 1962, and it developed rules for the sport for men and women. The first women's world championship meet was held in 1967.

World Cross-country Championships are still held once a year, with a junior race for competitors 19 and under and senior division for those 20 and up. Countries can send up to nine competitors, depending on the division.

Cross-country is also a popular high school sport. Over 400,000 high school students in the United States ran Cross-country in 2007, according to the National Federation of High School Athletics. The sport continues to draw additional competitors each year.

References

Appendix A:

Applegate, Liz, "The 15 foods runners need every week for good health and top performance," *Runner's World*, July 14, 2016. https://www.google.com/amp/s/www.runnersworld.com/nutrition/thebest-foods-for-runners%3famp/

Donnelly, Sean, "Diet guidelines for track and field runners," Stack.com, July 21, 2012. http://www.stack.com/a/track-and-field-guidelines

Fear, Craig, Fearless Eating: Traditional Food for Modern Times. https://fearlesseating.net/

iSport Track & Field, "How to maintain a healthy diet for track & field," n.d. http://track.isport.com/track-guides/how-to-maintain-a-healthy-diet-for-track-field

Appendix B:

Athnet, "Track and field history and the origins of the sport," Athnet.com, n.d. http://www.athleticscholarships.net/history-of-track-and-field.htm

"Cross-country running," Wikipedia. https://en.wikipedia.org/wiki/Cross_country_running

History, "April 6, 1896: First modern Olympic Games," History.com, n.d. http://www.history.com/thisday-in-history/first-modern-olympic-games

Jordan, Tom, "Track and field," Scholastic, n.d. https://www.scholastic.com/teachers/articles/teachingcontent/track-and-field/

Magness, Steve, "A brief history of track and field in the US," The Science of Running, n.d. http://www.scienceofrunning.com/2015/11/a-brief-history-of-track-and-field-in-the-us.html

Metzger, Justin, "A brief history of Cross-country," Indian Lake High School Cross-country, http://www.angelfire.com/oh5/jmetz/History.html

Robinson, Roger, "The origins of Cross-country," *Running Times*, Sept. 13, 2009. https://www.runnersworld.com/running-times-info/the-origins-of-cross-country

Tiefenthaler, David, "The history of Cross-country running," Tips4Running.com, n.d. http://www.tips4running.com/History-Of-Cross-Country.html

About the Author

Hi! I am Coach David Thompson. I have been a coach since 1993. I have coached at both the high school and college levels and enjoy it. I wrote this book to help coaches coordinate and organize their day-today practice and dual meet, so they can apply these criteria to themselves and their athletes.

I think education is important. I have my Associate degree in sports administration, a Personal Training Certification, and a Bachelor's degree in social and criminal justice. I am happily married with five lovely children, two of whom are adopted, so I have the determination to make a difference with my family as well as my community. I am pleased and happy to share this book with you. I hope you enjoy it. God bless and thank you.

College and University Track, Cross-country and Indoor
Attendance and Scorekeeping Information Log
by David E. Thompson

This is a Track and Field workbook that will help coaches and athletes coordinate and keep scores and statistics of dual meets and outdoor track, Cross-country, and indoor track and field. There are a number of illustrations and ideas that will help coaches and athletes manage or coordinate their practice and other activities. The research includes Track and Field Code of Ethics; attendance for all three-seasonal sports (track, Cross-country, and indoor); prayers for spiritual insight for coaches and athletes; diet and nutrition guidelines; and the history of track and field. This Track and Field Attendance and Scorekeeping Information Log is useful for college and university and for both men and women. This book will give all coaches the structure and understanding to coordinate and manage their day-to-day practice and dual meets and will help them envision their daily track and field preparation.

There is a coach survey evaluation form that coaches should present to athletes at the end of the season. Coaches can use the evaluation form from the athlete's feedback to create a better program for the following year.

Printed in the United States
By Bookmasters